The Declaration of Independence

Jill K. Mulhall, M. Ed.

Table of Contents

Words That Changed the World

When the colonists in America decided to declare independence from Great Britain, their leaders knew they needed a special document. It would explain all the reasons they were willing to take this big step. A young man named Thomas Jefferson wrote a beautiful essay. It inspired people to change the world.

What Should We Do Next?

The people in America were loyal British citizens (SIT-uh-zuhns) for many years. But in the middle of the 1700s things changed. The people did not like how their leaders across the sea treated them. They began to object to taxes and laws that they thought were unfair.

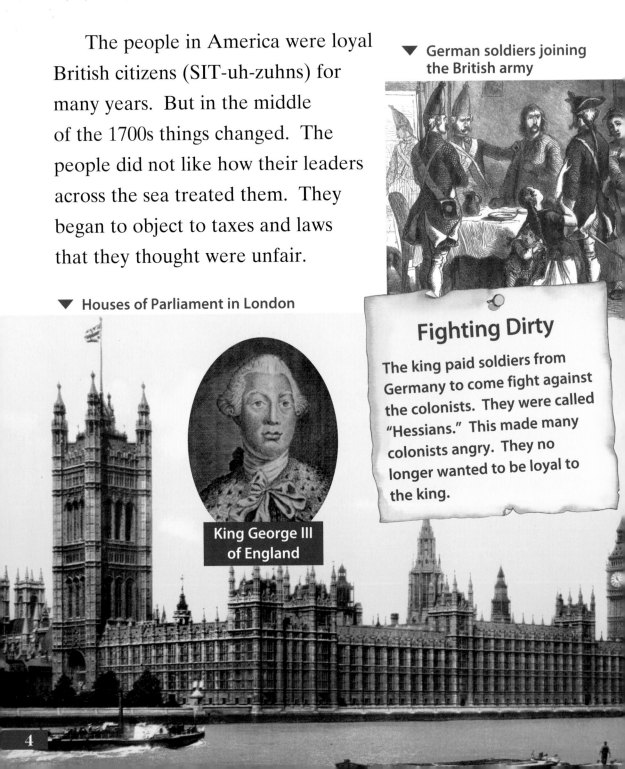

▼ German soldiers joining the British army

▼ Houses of Parliament in London

King George III of England

Fighting Dirty

The king paid soldiers from Germany to come fight against the colonists. They were called "Hessians." This made many colonists angry. They no longer wanted to be loyal to the king.

Revolutionary battle in Pennsylvania

Surprising Victories

At first many colonists believed there was no way they could win a war against Great Britain. But the colonial military surprised them. It did very well early in the war. The colonists began to believe that maybe they could actually win.

Britain's Parliament (PAR-luh-muhnt) and King George III did not handle this problem well. Sometimes they ignored the colonists' complaints. Other times they were too harsh with the people.

By 1775, the colonists were so angry that they were willing to go to war. The battles of the American Revolution began in April.

The war had begun. But the people were still not sure exactly what they were fighting for. Some of them just wanted their faraway leaders to respect their rights. Others wanted to be free from Great Britain once and for all.

▲ Meeting of the Continental Congress

▲ Olive branch

A Peaceful Petition

The message sent to the king was called the Olive Branch Petition (puh-TISH-uhn). The olive branch is a very old symbol for peace. Congress was trying to tell the king that they did not want to fight.

Getting Close to a Decision

The colonists asked their leaders to help them decide what to do next. They sent delegates to Philadelphia for the Second Continental (kon-tuh-NEN-tuhl) Congress.

At first, most of the delegates thought that the colonists should remain British citizens. They even sent King George a message that told him they were still loyal. But the king would not even read it. He called the people in the colonies traitors.

The delegates began to think that liberty was their only choice. They talked about the details for many months.

In June 1776, a delegate named Richard Henry Lee got up to speak. He proposed that Congress finally declare independence from Great Britain. A few men still thought this was a bad idea. But most of the delegates agreed with Lee. They decided to vote on the idea a few weeks later.

Congress thought it should prepare a document. The document would explain the reasons the colonists wanted freedom. Having it ready would save time when the big decision was made at last.

▼ This document is the Lee Resolution, which proposes that Congress declare independence.

A Special Landmark

Congress met in the Old Pennsylvania State House. By the time they finished their important work, this building had a new name. From then on it was known as Independence Hall.

An Important Task

Congress chose a committee of five men to write the declaration. Four of them were from the North. Their names were John Adams, Benjamin Franklin, Robert Livingston, and Roger Sherman. The only southerner was a quiet delegate from Virginia named Thomas Jefferson.

The committee met to discuss how to handle this important job. They decided it would be too hard to write as a group. Instead they decided to have one person write the essay. Then they would all meet to go over it together.

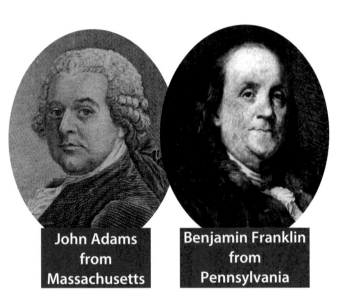

John Adams from Massachusetts

Benjamin Franklin from Pennsylvania

Roger Sherman from Connecticut

Robert Livingston from New York

Different Viewpoints

Each of the men on the committee was from a different colony. Congress did this on purpose. They wanted points of view from many areas to be included.

Jefferson had written some important papers in the past. The committee knew he was a gifted writer. So, they chose him to write the document.

The group told Jefferson three things he had to write about. He had to describe what makes a good government. Then, he had to explain why King George had not done a good job. Finally, he had to announce that the colonists were declaring themselves free of Great Britain.

Flattery Will Get You Everywhere

At first Thomas Jefferson did not want to write the declaration. He thought John Adams should do it. But Adams talked Jefferson into it. He said, "You can write ten times better than I can."

Thomas Jefferson from Virginia

The Declaration of Independence committee:
Roger Sherman, Thomas Jefferson, Benjamin Franklin,
▼ John Adams, and Robert Livingston

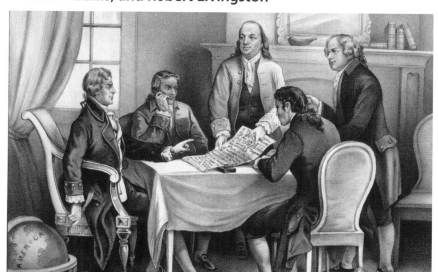

The Right Man for the Job

The committee made a smart choice when it picked Thomas Jefferson to write the document. He was a great writer. He was also very excited about the subject.

Jefferson worked as a lawyer back in Virginia. But he was interested in many things besides the law. He read books for hours every day. Many of them were about politics and history. These books made Jefferson do a lot of thinking.

He also liked to hear people debate. He was shy and did not always speak up himself. But he learned a lot by listening.

Jefferson came to believe that freedom was something that people could not live without. He was happy when the other members of Congress finally agreed with him.

For more than two weeks, Jefferson worked on his essay. During that time, he rarely spoke to anyone. He used all his energy to write. He wanted the words to be so powerful that everyone would agree with them.

Family Matters

It was hard for Jefferson to concentrate on his writing. His baby daughter and his mother had recently died. His wife, Martha, was very sick. Jefferson wanted to be home in Virginia to take care of her.

Better on Paper

When Jefferson was young he wanted to become a great speaker. He even practiced giving speeches in front of a mirror. But his voice was too soft. He was not exciting to watch. So he became known for his writing instead.

▲ Jefferson's early draft of the Declaration of Independence

A Natural Place to Start

Jefferson began his paper by explaining its important purpose. Many people still thought it was foolish to declare independence from Great Britain. This essay would explain to the world why the colonists deserved freedom.

First, he stated that all people are born with equal rights. Everyone deserves the same basic freedoms . And nobody should ever take those things away. This sounds normal to us now. But in 1776 it was a new and exciting idea.

Jefferson invented this ▶
special writing desk.
He used it to write the
Declaration of Independence.

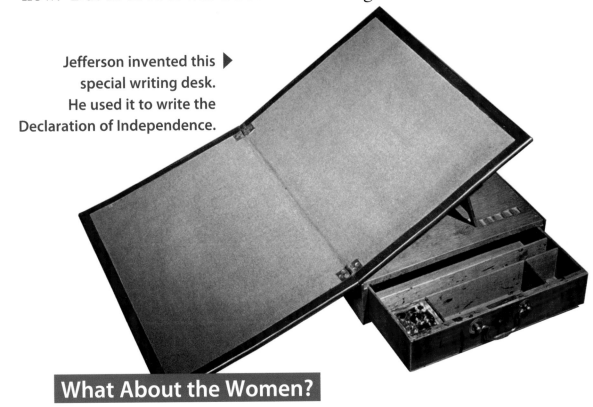

What About the Women?

Jefferson wrote, "all men are created equal." But he did not mention women. Most people did not think much about women's rights then. But when we read the document now we know that it speaks for all people.

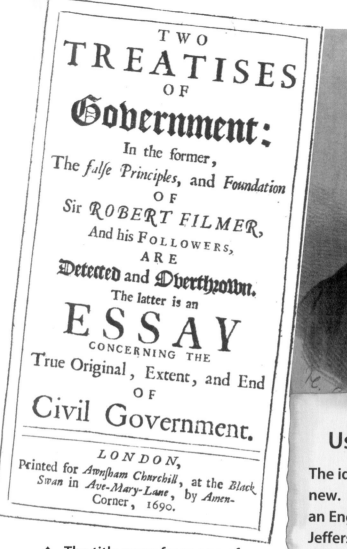

The title page from one of John Locke's essays

Using Locke's Ideas

The idea of natural rights was not new. It came from the writings of an Englishman named John Locke. Jefferson had studied his work for many years.

Then, he explained that natural rights are, "life, liberty, and the pursuit of happiness." It would be pretty hard to disagree with those.

Finally, Jefferson explained that a government had one main job. It had to help the people get and keep their basic rights. If it did not do this, it had failed. Then, the people would have the right to rebel.

Strong Words for the King

The first section of the Declaration of Independence stated that people deserve a government that protects their rights. In the second part, the paper described Britain's government. It explained how the government had failed to do its job in the colonies.

Jefferson wrote that King George III had done an unforgivable thing. He had kept the people from making decisions about how to live their own lives.

Cartoon showing America as a horse throwing off King George ▼

Propaganda

Some of the complaints against the king were fair. But others were a bit exaggerated. Jefferson wanted to get people angry with the king. That way they would support independence.

There was a long list of complaints against the king. Some described how he had taken away people's rights. Others told how he had put colonists in danger. A few mentioned how he had cost them money. Jefferson used very strong words. He made the king sound as bad as he could.

Letting Them Off the Hook

Jefferson also wrote about the regular citizens of Great Britain. He complained that they had not helped the people in America. Later, Congress took out this part. They did not want to make the British people angry.

▼ King George III of England

▲ The original 13 colonies became the first states of the new country created by the Declaration of Independence.

Leaving the Old World Behind

The final section of the paper contained some remarkable thoughts. First, it pointed out that the colonists had tried many times to let King George know about their unhappiness. Each time the king had ignored them. So, Jefferson called the king a tyrant. This was a very bold thing to say.

Then, it declared that the colonists would no longer be British citizens. They would not be loyal to a king who had done such a bad job. In fact, they would no longer have any political ties to Great Britain.

Instead, they would form a new country called the United States of America. This country would have all the powers of any other nation.

This was an amazing thing to declare. At that time, all countries were run by a few powerful rulers. People had never thought that the citizens could create their own government.

The Age of Revolution

This essay inspired people all over the world. They liked the idea of the citizens running things themselves. Soon after, the king of France refused to listen to his people. They beheaded him and took over the government.

Beheading King Louis XVI of France ▲

In Over His Head

Calling King George a tyrant was a good way to get the king's attention. But it was not really true. The king was not cruel. In fact, most people thought he was nice. He was just not very good at his job.

Proud of His Work

Thomas Jefferson went on to do many important things in his life. He even became the third president of the United States. But the thing he was always most proud of was writing the Declaration of Independence.

A Most Important Vote

When Jefferson finished his essay, he showed it to the committee. They were very happy with his work. They made some changes to the wording. But they felt he had done a good job of explaining all the important ideas.

On June 28, the committee presented Jefferson's rough draft to Congress. The delegates were pleased with the document. They decided that now was the time to make a final decision about whether to declare independence.

They spent the next few days in more debate. Finally, on July 2, it was time to vote. The proposal passed in a landslide. Jefferson's words had inspired the delegates. They had done something the world had never seen before.

The committee reviews Jefferson's draft of the Declaration of Independence

One State Was Late

Twelve of the 13 colonies voted to declare independence on July 2. Only New York abstained. The New York delegates were still waiting to hear what their state wanted them to do. A week later they finally got word to vote yes.

◀ Congress debates the issues

Preparing a Final Draft

Congress spent two days reviewing Jefferson's rough draft. They made many small changes.

There was, however, one very important change. In one long section, Jefferson had criticized Great Britain for trading slaves. The southern colonies refused to include this part. They made Congress remove it from the final document.

▲ Trading slaves in the colonies

Signature Slang

Do you know what it means if someone asks for your "John Hancock"? It means they want you to sign your name. Now, you know where that term comes from.

▲ John Hancock's signature on the Declaration of Independence

Risking Everything

Signing the Declaration was a brave thing to do. If the United States had lost the Revolutionary War, the signers would have been arrested. Then they could have been hanged as traitors.

On July 4, 1776, Congress voted to ratify the final version of the Declaration. This is why we celebrate Independence Day on the fourth of July. John Hancock was the president of the Congress so he signed first. He wrote his name in big, bold letters. He wanted King George to be able to read it without putting on his glasses!

In August, Congress held a formal signing of the Declaration of Independence. It had been copied onto special paper. In the end, 56 delegates put their names on this historic document.

Spreading the News

▲ The first reading of the Declaration of Independence

Congress wanted the people to see the Declaration as soon as possible. So they made many handwritten copies. These were sent to all 13 colonies.

The first public reading was in Philadelphia on July 8. A huge crowd listened to the important words. Then, they set off fireworks and lit bonfires to celebrate. Does this remind you of what Americans do on the Fourth of July every summer?

George Washington ordered the document read to all his troops. It inspired the soldiers. Now, they could say exactly what they were fighting for.

The Declaration of Independence helped change the world. People decided that they deserved more say in their lives. The document still moves people who read it today. It inspires them to fight for equal rights. That is pretty amazing for words written more than 225 years ago.

A New Use for the King

A crowd in New York got excited when they heard the Declaration of Independence. They pulled down a heavy metal statue of King George. Then, they melted it and made more than 40,000 bullets.

An Amazing Coincidence

Thomas Jefferson lived for exactly 50 years after his Declaration was approved. He died on July 4, 1826. John Adams, who had talked Jefferson into writing it, died that exact same day.

Glossary

abstained—did not vote either yes or no

beheaded—cut off someone's head

citizens—people who are members of a country and receive protection from it in return

committee—a group that is created to do a specific task

Continental Congress—government meetings of the colonists in America

debate—talking about both sides of an idea

declaration—a formal announcement

delegates—people who are sent to a meeting to speak for a larger group of people

document—an official paper

independence—standing on your own, without help from anyone

landslide—a really big victory

liberty—freedom

natural—something that comes automatically instead of being made by people

Parliament—group that makes the laws in Great Britain

pursuit—chasing after

ratify—make official

rebel—fight back against someone in charge

symbol—something used to represent the real thing

traitors—people who betray their country

tyrant—a ruler who is very harsh and cruel to his people